LIKE MY FATHER ALWAYS SAID . . .

ERIN McHUGH

LIKE MY FATHER ALWAYS SAID . . .

GRUFF ADVICE, SWEET WISDOM, AND
HALF-BAKED INSTRUCTIONS ON HOW
TO FIX YOUR STUFF AND YOUR LIFE

ERIN McHUGH

ABRAMS IMAGE
NEW YORK

Editor: David Cashion
Designer: Devin Grosz
Production Manager: Denise LaCongo

Library of Congress Control Number: 2014945995

ISBN: 978-1-4197-1621-8

Printed and bound in the United States
10 9 8 7 6 5 4 3 2 1

Abrams Image books are available at special discounts
when purchased in quantity for premiums and promotions
as well as fundraising or educational use. Special editions
can also be created to specification. For details, contact
specialsales@abramsbooks.com or the address below.

THE ART OF BOOKS SINCE 1949
115 West 18th Street
New York, NY 10011
www.abramsbooks.com

To my father,
James Francis McHugh,
who thought I hung the moon.

"You're a champion!"

– JIM McHUGH, father of ERIN

CONTENTS

INTRODUCTION

A year ago I sent out the smoke signal (well, OK, the e-mails, texts, Facebook and Twitter shout-outs) to everyone—and then they sent it on to everybody they knew—to start collecting quips and anecdotes and advice they all remembered receiving from their mothers. It was both a fun and bittersweet adventure. Many of our mothers were gone, and the recounting of these stories brought back memories for all of us, and even the tales that weren't our own had a familiar ring. But readers loved the trip—it was like a visit with your mother, and the other mothers you knew, all over again.

And then soon enough I found that a lot of the contributors to that book, called *Like My Mother Always Said . . . Wise Words, Witty Warnings, and Odd Advice We Never Forget*, had something else to say: "But don't you want to know what my dad said?!" Well, yes I did! So, I started to listen, because I was curious. I wasn't even sure moms and dads would sound that different from each other—but did they ever! What I started to hear from sons and daughters about their fathers was altogether different from what we called the "Momisms."

If I had to make a sweeping generalization? I'd say mothers more often are watching out that you don't run with scissors, eat too much candy, or fall off the roof. While all that's going on, your dad is busy thinking about a firm handshake, your 401(k), and the worthiness of your future spouse. Mothers' love is out there for all to see; Dad is gruff, but with a soft spot you could drive a truck through. And perhaps the "Dadisms" within this book are a product of the times. Contributors are, for the most part, adults, having grown up when mothers—even if they were also working outside the home—were in charge of the house and most of the child rearing; fathers were working in the world, bringing home the bacon, and observing what the changes would be like out there when their children grew up and set out.

So are each parent's observations different? Well, you'll hear more about changing your oil and checking the tires from fathers, but also about ambition, and job equality for sons and daughters.

But you can count on one thing that's always the same, for fathers and mothers around the world—and that's the love. So read on, and revel in it.

Erin McHugh
New York City, September 2014

I

MY DAD CAN DO ANYTHING

Who do you look up to more as a kid than your dad? He's a mountain man, a genius, a great pitcher, taller and faster than your friends' dads. He can do anything, that's for sure. And by the time you find out that maybe that's not exactly accurate . . . it really doesn't matter anymore.

Daddy never said much, but he could yodel with the best of them. He was raised a Missouri farm boy but he was a cowboy in his heart, ridin' the range, ropin' dogies. My cradle songs were "Red River Valley" and "Tumbling Tumbleweeds"; he told endless bedtime stories about Jed Thumper, a giant jackrabbit who was always up to no good and bore not the slightest resemblance to his distant cousin Peter; my heroes were Roy Rogers and Gene Autry and we'd have long, serious discussions about which one was really the King of the Cowboys.

– JAYNE, daughter of Ferrell

"DO IT RIGHT OR DO IT AGAIN."

– NORM, father of Erik

> "Why are you stressed?
> I don't get stressed. People get
> stressed and I'm not people.
> I don't get ulcers, I give them."

– JOHN, father of John

My dad was a Navy Seal, so he had no tolerance for his daughters' whining or complaining. He used to say the only time we might be able to miss school for pain or illness would be "if your arm was cut off and hanging by a thread." Anything more minor than that, well then, off to school we would go. He also loved to use the Navy Seal motto, "The only easy day was yesterday," to remind us to face our daily challenges and to keep on truckin' (yes, it was the seventies).

– JENNIFER, daughter of Barry

Whenever my father was working on a project that didn't come out quite as well as he hoped, he'd sigh and say, "Good enough for government work."

– JAMES, son of James

"Any man ever gives you any guff, just get yourself a two-by-four full of rusty nails . . . and give 'em a good raking with it."

– JAKE, father of Kate

My dad was a mechanic by trade—and a good one at that. He knew how to diagnose a problem and then correct that problem without needless delay or excessive parts replacement. He was so good he could even diagnose a problem over the phone. One of the things he told me when I was getting my driver's license was that he really didn't care very much if I could start the car. The most important thing with a car is if you can stop it. I was sixteen and thought he was crazy. But if you really think about it, he was so very right.

– TOM, son of Henry

I've been in the book industry my entire adult life, so I probably shouldn't admit this, but I don't really remember reading in bed at night as a little kid. Nor do I remember my parents reading to me in my pj's. But that's because I have another memory that most kids do not. My dad and I sang torch songs instead.

After I got in bed, my father would come up and give me a back rub, and then we would start to sing: Sinatra standards, Irish songs, show tunes. We sang in rounds, we excelled at duets, and harmony—well, we killed at harmonizing and always did, even when I grew up.

Give me "Rosie O'Grady," "The Good Life," "Lida Rose," "Show Me the Way to Go Home"— name it, I knew every word to these songs and more, and remember them all still. What can I say? We virtually sang our way through my childhood. When I worried about being smart enough, popular enough, whether I'd get on the team, I always knew how my day would end. It's my favorite memory of growing up.

– ERIN, daughter of Jimmy

"THOSE OF YOU WHO ARE STANDING AROUND SAYING IT CAN'T BE DONE ARE BOTHERING THOSE OF US WHO ARE DOING IT."

– DEWEY, father of Jean

2

DISTRACTION, AVOIDANCE, AND REDIRECTION

Ever notice how fathers have a certain way of avoiding the subject if they need to? When you were a kid, you took what your dad said as gospel, but as you began to grow up, you found yourself occasionally thinking, "Heeeey, wait a minute! What th'. . ."

Whenever there might be a potential squabble looming among us siblings, Dad would look over his newspaper at the three of us and ask, "What do you know about freight trains?" We'd be so busy trying to figure out the answer to his question that we forgot about our argument. Dad would go back to reading his paper and we three kids continued to play while discussing freight trains.

– DENISE, MARC, AND PAUL, children of Marcel

On the occasion he was asked how frequently he had sex, my father always said, "How many times a week is semiannual?"

– SHELLEY, stepdaughter of Joe

My dad disliked eating in restaurants with low lighting. He felt it didn't allow you to see your food properly, and when we'd end up in one he'd always say, "What's this, a cheater's joint?"

– CHRIS, daughter of Andy

"GET EVEN BY SELLING THEM."

– ARTHUR, father of Allan

When we were little and my parents entertained, my father would mix cocktails and we kids would deliver them to the guests. My dad would punctuate these special deliveries with, "Midget waiters! Makes the drinks look bigger!"

– LEO, son of Bud

Any time you asked my father to do something he didn't want to do, he'd say, "I'm afraid I can't do that. I've got a bone in my leg."

– BRYAN, son of Carl

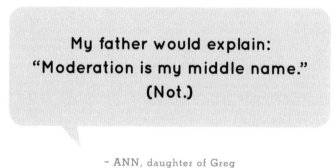

My father would explain: "Moderation is my middle name." (Not.)

– ANN, daughter of Greg

My father always would say, when something scary happened to the family, like a serious illness that ended up coming out good, "Well, we dodged a bullet!"

– LIZA, daughter of Orville

"IF YOU CAN'T GO ONE
WAY, GO THE OTHER."

– HENRY, grandfather of Josie

"GIVE ME ANOTHER DRINK,
I CAN STILL HEAR THE KIDS."

– SAM, father of Michael

When my mother would send
me to wake up my dad, he would
say, "I can't pop out of bed like
a piece of warm toast."

– MARY, daughter of Bob

My dad always said, "Every day is Christmas." You see, his name was Natale Felice, which means Merry Christmas. He was born on Christmas Day.

– TOM, son of Tom (né Natale Felice)

On getting an after-school/ summer job: "It puts money in your pocket and keeps you out of trouble."

– RAUL, father of Raul

"Take a Sunday afternoon car ride to blow the stink off."

– ROY, father of Doug

If my dad didn't want you to know what he was talking about or what he was doing, he'd say, "Winnermaus." He said it meant "none of your business" in German.

– PATRICIA, daughter of Joe

On interaction with the authorities: "You're all right if they don't take your name."

– BERRY, father of Eliza

If asked what he was doing— when it was completely obvious—my dad would crack, "Writing a letter."

– DONNA, daughter of John

"DO WHATEVER YOU WANT TO DO—FIGURE IT OUT AND I WILL EXPLAIN IT TO MOM LATER."

– BOB, father of Robin

3

GROWING UP RIGHT

How many times did you hear by the time you turned eighteen that there was a right way and a wrong way for just about every situation on earth? Saving money. Manners. Telling the truth. And yes, returning that thing you stole from the store. By the time you had a chance to do things your own way, damn if maybe the way you were taught wasn't the best way after all.

For my twelfth birthday, my father gave me a book, personalized with an inscription:

"Your Bible is the most important and treasured book that you have—may *this* one be a pleasure to you during all the years of your life."

It was a copy of Emily Post's *Etiquette*. I thought it an odd choice for a gift at the time, but it turns out it was perfect.

– NANCY, daughter of Walter

"Honesty is not the best policy. It's the only policy."

– CREATH, father of Chuck

"Don't confuse liberty with license!"

– JIM, father of Susie

"I want you to go out there and give it 150 percent!"
A little pressure, but not the worst advice for life.

– JOYCE, daughter of Burt

> ## "DON'T EVER THINK YOU ARE BETTER THAN ANOTHER PERSON."

– EDWARD, father of Tina

My dad would say, "Before speaking, you should think about what you're going to say for at least ten seconds. Then, hopefully, you'll say nothing." I actually still follow this advice; it drives my wife crazy.

– DOUG, son of Steve

"Always acknowledge a kindness."

– GEORGE, father of Michelle

My dad loved a game—any kind of game, whether it was tennis, golf, horseshoes, or penny ante poker. And though he just hated to lose, he was a guy who insisted on playing by the rules. In fact, the first fight he and my mom ever had was about playing croquet, and the proper regulations on "sending" the ball.

This old saying evidently was fairly common back in the day, but we actually had a very dog-eared copy of *Hoyle's Rules of Games*, which was kept on our coffee table. So it wasn't unusual for Dad to say, if anyone questioned the righteousness of anything, whether it was a game or not: "It's strictly according to *Hoyle's*!"

– ERIN, daughter of Jim

"DON'T OVERNEGOTIATE."

– BERNARD, father of Linda

"When you surround yourself with good people and work hard, good things happen."

– DICK, grandfather of Tommy

"WHY WOULD YOU BUY BOTTLED WATER? IT COSTS MORE THAN SCOTCH!"

– JAMES, father of Jancee

"So you're at an age now and free enough so that I can't stop you from doing anything you might want to do. Just remember that you always have a choice and can choose to not do anything stupid."

– BOB, father of Bob

"There is only one thing that you can both keep and give: your word."

– CASEY, father of Peter and Paul

"Manners go a long way and they don't cost a dime."

– DICK, father of Dick Jr. and Patty

"You can have as much freedom as you can pay for."

– IRVING, father of Greg

My father was an amateur handyman around the house, which is no doubt where I got my willingness to jump into home projects. One thing he always said was, "Measure twice, cut once!" I live by this little saying in all things in life.

– HOWIE, son of Ted

"Never miss an opportunity to cross out an unnecessary comma."

– SCOTT, father of Genny and Dave

"There's a right way to do something and that's that. Why do it the wrong way when the right way lets you do it once?"

– SONNY, father of Tim

"If you don't invest very much, then defeat doesn't hurt very much and winning is not very exciting."

– DICK, grandfather of Tommy

"If you can't do something gracefully, don't do it at all."

– BILL, father of Kellie

"Would you rather be right or be kind?"

– FRED, father of Dylan

My dad was a special agent of the FBI and a helluva smart guy. He advised my brother, my sister, and me for decades in our respective careers in the law, business, and publishing and we were smart to follow his advice. To my dad, well-crafted letters were the go-to form of communication and he was always urging us to put our thoughts—particularly our praise of others—in writing.

It pays off every time:

"Fire off a letter."

"Shoot him a note."

"Memo the chief."

"Write her an 'attaboy.'"

"Bullet-point the particulars."

Will do, Dad. And I'll "cc" the file.

> – JOANIE, daughter of Bill

"Be good, even if it hurts."

> – JIM, father of Joan

"YOUR ONLY RESPONSIBILITY IN LIFE IS TO BE KIND."

– FREDDIE, father of Marion

4

FATHERLY
ADVICE

The world has changed a lot in the last couple of decades, but back when a lot of us were kids, Mom was holding down the fort at home, and Dad was out there fighting the good fight and bringing back news from the front. He had a million suggestions about how to avoid getting steamrolled by life; he was always there to pass on advice, from both victories and defeats.

My father was incredibly disciplined and result-oriented, and he tried to pass on those qualities to us. When I expressed some wish to do something or achieve something or complained that it wasn't possible, he would say, "You can do anything you want if you make up your mind. The hard part is making up your mind."

My sibs and I repeat this still, and often in unison.

– DENISE, daughter of George

"Never back down from a bully."

– TOM, father of Meredith

My dad, driving around one day while I was reading *In Cold Blood* for the first time, said, "If anyone ever breaks into your home and tries to tie you up, say no. If they're cowards, they will back down and you have a better chance of surviving. If they're going to kill you, they will anyway. At least if you say no, you're giving yourself a chance."

– KAYLIE, daughter of author James Jones

Every time my sisters and I got upset about an unexpected shift in our lives: "Don't sweat it."

– JEAN, daughter of Wayne

"IF THE REASON CEASES, SO TOO SHALL THE RULE."

– RICHARD, father of Deborah

"It doesn't worth it." My father was a man who spoke very little English, but managed to form the perfect blend of "It's not worth it" and "It doesn't really matter."

– LESLIE, daughter of Al

"Your attitude determines your altitude."

– PETER, father of Sam

"Keep your head down and stay the course."

– ROBERT, father of Christina

Whether I was at a crossroad of a decision or leaving the house as a young woman exploring the world, Dad would offer two words of advice: "*Soyez prudent.*" Be prudent. I tucked Dad's words away in a vault in my mind. When I had my own three children, Dad's wisdom found its home in my heart. "*Soyez prudent*" took on a whole new meaning. I still remember those two words when I make important decisions.

– DENISE, daughter of Marcel

"You can't argue by yourself."

– JOHN, father of Danny

"Check your oil and tires once a week."

– JACK, father of Anne

"THERE ARE MORE TIDES THAN SAILORS," DAD SAID, WHICH MEANT THERE WILL ALWAYS BE ANOTHER CHANCE.

– RAQUEL, daughter of Daniel

So the night before my first day at E. F. Hutton, my dad took me to a Rangers game. We had great seats, right up on the glass, and it was an exciting game with lots of fighting. That's all I remember, because my dad turned to me at one point and said, "Now I'm going to share the secret of success with you and I want you to listen." He went on to say, "There are three things I want you to do. First, and this is the most important, be nice to everyone you meet, especially secretaries and receptionists. Say 'good morning' and 'please' and 'thank you' and ask them about their weekend and their families. Second, work hard and you'll get ahead. Always get in before your boss and leave after she leaves." Yes, he said "she"! "Third, learn the job of the person on your left and the person on your right. One day one of them will quit and the work will need to get done and you will be there to volunteer to do it." As my mom would say, "Truer words were never spoke!" I did as I was told and the rest is history. I share his story with every training class I speak to. It's been thirty-plus years and still the best career advice I have ever heard.

– SHELLEY, daughter of Marty

"The only bad mistake is one you stick by."

– LOU, father of Sally

"Work like a horse, eat like a horse."

– HENRY, grandfather of Josie

"Don't just stand there with your bare
face hanging out. Do something!"

– STANLEY, father of Lucia

"YOU'RE ENTITLED TO YOUR
OPINION, BUT YOU DON'T
GET YOUR OWN FACTS."

– MARIO, father of Elisa

"Worry about the elephants, not the rabbits."

– MARK, father of Elizabeth

"Only a fool makes assumptions and then acts upon them as if they were fact."

– RAOUL, father of Nanette

"Better to have and not need than need and not have."

– LAWRENCE, father of Lydia

"Stay with the plan." Sounds easy, but my parents started their own business over fifty years ago, and every time someone suggested a diversification, or they were tempted to try something else, Dad came back to that self-imposed rule over and over again. And now, the third generation is "staying with the plan."

– ANN, daughter of Jack

My dad told us (his three daughters) to pick a profession with a name—a doctor, a lawyer, a teacher, a nurse—because you can always get a good job when no one needs an explanation to understand what it is that you do. He was a credit manager. Bet you don't know what a credit manager does, do you? Also, he told us to marry a dentist: all the prestige of a doctor, no emergency calls in the middle of the night.

So, I'm a lawyer, and both of my sisters are nurses. None of us married dentists.

– SHARON, daughter of Stuart

"Before you speak: Is it kind? Is it true? Is it necessary?"

– DAVE, father of Wendy

"Excel."

— DON, stepfather of Kalen

I had just received early acceptance letters from three good colleges, and wasn't sure what direction to go . . . law, medicine, or art. My dad was aware of my conundrum, and invited me to lunch at the Baltimore Museum of Art. That's when he imparted this sage bit of advice that I think I've passed along to others at least half a dozen times: "Do what you love." It was so simple, yet it resonated deeply with me. His reasoning was, "You're (hopefully) going to make a career out of what you study, and will be doing it for the rest of your life . . . so, choose something you're passionate about. Do what you love." I've followed his advice ever since, and it hasn't failed me yet! And, yes, I chose art!

Sly of him to have chosen the BMA for our lunch!

— LAURIE, daughter of Gardner

"KEEP IT SIMPLE."

– JACK, father of Nancy

5

THE
FACTS
OF LIFE

At some point, your father sat you down and said, "Let me tell you the facts of life." And guess what: It wasn't the talk about the birds and the bees, it was the one about what a friend is; how to avoid people who might manipulate you; how you'll know you're in love. If you forgot to listen up, here's a little review.

"Just don't be 'that kid.' Whatever the situation, you never want to be the one everyone else refers to as 'Oh yeah, I know that kid.' It's never good."

– KEITH, father of Connor

My dad had a very stressful job at Macy's and was swimming with sharks, so he had to learn to be cutthroat or risk having his throat cut! One of the sayings he often repeated was based on his "kill or be killed" philosophy: "What's bad for me and bad for you is bad. What's bad for me and good for you is really bad. If it's good for both of us, then that's OK. But if it's good for me and bad for you, then that's the best!"

– ANNE, daughter of Albert

"People can always do what they want, they just have to want to do it; they can always find a way."

– J.D., father of Randy

My parents built a very successful business of their own but, of course, the ups and downs were always on their heads. After a slow day at work, my father would say, "It's so quiet I can hear the overhead rising."

– NANCY, daughter of Jack

"Worry about the things you can change. Don't worry about the things you can't."

– DON, father of Mary

"Look with your eyes, not with your mouth!" my father would say in response to us kids yelling, "Has anybody seen my . . ."

– KIKI, daughter of Donald

My father grew up on some rough New York City streets and he was a very shrewd businessman. He always told me when selling something, "Your first offer is your best offer. Sell or be sorry."

– SANDY, daughter of Plutarch

"Drink only one beer at a time."

– DAN, father of Annie

"You've got to network," said my dad, constantly, ever since I entered the workforce.

– BETH, daughter of Martin

"Never let the sun set on your anger. Life is too short for negative emotions to linger."

– CASIMIRE, father of Charlie

"No is a complete sentence."

– BRUCE, father of John

My father was an obstetrician. When presented by a proud patient with a particularly odd-looking infant, he would always say, "Now, *that's* a baby!"

– MICHAEL, son of Peter

"Get an education. It's the only
thing they can't take from you."

– DOC, grandfather of M.

"If you let the small jobs add up,
they become big jobs."

– JIM, father of Tracy

My dad, when faced with a defect or a
mistake, would say, "A blind man on a
galloping horse will never see it."

– MICHAEL, son of George

"Ain't nothing free."

– JAMES, father of Dinah

"THE SQUEAKY WHEEL GETS REPLACED."

– JACK, father of Ann

My dad gave me three pieces of advice when I got my first "real" job:

Always max out your 401(k) contribution.

Always change the oil in your car at 3,000 miles.

Always read the sports section so you have something to add to a conversation.

– JOAN, daughter of Dewey

"There's always a little bit of truth in sarcasm."

– PETER, father of Ruth

Me: "Dad, why did you cancel my allowance for this week? I said I would clean up my room later."

Dad: "We promise according to our hopes but perform according to our fears."

– DAN, son of Clare

My father, the colonel, used to say to me and my brother before we would go out at night in the naval town of Newport, Rhode Island, "Be careful now, and watch out for the militia!" The following morning as we lay there nursing our hangovers he would say, "Ya know boys, if you're going to hoot with the owls at night, you're not going to fly with the eagles in the morning!"

– GREG, son of Frank

"Ya can't fix stupid."

– BILL, father of Martha

"IF HE'S NOT CRAZY ABOUT YOU BEFORE YOU GET MARRIED, HE DEFINITELY WILL NOT BE AFTERWARDS."

– DIXON, father of Dini

"Being a Red Sox fan prepares you for every disappointment in life."

– GREG, father of Martha

"Never take for granted having
a good roof over your head."

– PETE, father of Sally

"YOU CAN'T PLOW POTATOES AND LOOK AT THE STARS."

– ARTHUR, father of Edmée

My dad's thoughts when I wondered if I
should major in business instead of art so
I could get a good job:

Dad: "Are you passionate about business?"

Me: "Not really, but I could make money."

Dad: "You won't be any good at it and
probably won't make a damn cent."

– HILDA, daughter of Doc

"Stay single! But if you're going to get married, get married in the morning. Because then if it doesn't work out, you haven't wasted the whole day."

– BOB, father of Dick

"Enjoy your youth. Because after forty, what happens to everyone? General decrepitation."

– ABE, father of Marti

"I don't care if a man is black or white as long he carries the potatoes."

– DOC, grandfather of M.

"If you can read, you can do anything."

– BILL, father of Deborah

When someone would do something underhanded at work, my father would say, "It's not that they are against you. It is just that they are so for themselves."

– VALERIE, daughter of Chuck

"Make sure you learn at least one new thing every day."

– BOB, father of Lisa

"Nix is for nix," Dad said,
meaning, "Nothing is for free."

– BILL, son of Franz

On the occasion of buying my first apartment, I was distracted by a building that had a gorgeous lobby and a so-so apartment. My father's observation: "You don't sleep in the lobby."

– MARY, daughter of Bill

"NEVER TRUST ANYONE WHO SAYS, 'TRUST ME.'"

– HAL, father of Brad

LIFE LESSONS AND OBSERVATIONS

"All you have to do in life is be this much smarter than an a**hole."

"Only bums don't wear undershirts."

Regarding eating well: "There are a finite amount of meals in this life."

"Stupid and lazy is a bad combination."

"The amount of money you steal determines whether they build you a monument or throw you in jail."

"Tuesday's the only day anyone does any work. Maybe, Wednesday morning."

– ANTHONY, father of Deena and Peter

"BURNS TEACH."

– DON, father of Stephen

"DON'T MAKE A DECISION UNTIL YOU HAVE TO, BUT HAVE IT READY WHEN YOU HAVE TO MAKE IT."

– TOM, father of Tom

6

NONSENSE AND PALAVER

OK, so maybe not all of Dad's nuggets of knowledge are useful. Some are nutty and old-fashioned. Plenty of stuff just sounds like he ran out of steam. But the funny part is, he truly believes it all. He probably should get points just for that.

Here's what my dad, Bob, said to my husband, Randy, at our wedding before walking me down the aisle: "Are you sure you know what you are getting into? Cindy's expensive. I just got finished paying for her." Randy was already like a deer in the headlights about getting married. Not knowing my dad's sense of humor, you can imagine his not knowing what to make of it. I of course rebutted that "you get what you pay for, and I am worth it." Having just graduated from grad school and in debt up to my eyeballs, I knew my dad was right! Randy still married me.

— CINDY, daughter of Bob

"If you haven't done what you're going to do by midnight, you shouldn't be doing it."

— LARRY, father of Beth

> # "I WASN'T ASLEEP. I WAS JUST CHECKING OUT THE INSIDE OF MY EYELIDS."

– ROBERT, father of Christina

When I was a kid, my dad always carried a little extra "poundage." After a snack—or any meal— he would also drink a big glass of orange juice and then declare, "Orange juice cuts the fat!"

– BARB, daughter of Bob

"The bit of mold on the bread won't kill you. After all, penicillin is made from mold."

– LAWRENCE, father of Lisa

"Nothing happens when you stay home."

– HAROLD, father of Susan

"If my aunt had wheels, she'd be a bus."
That would be his response to any sentence
you might say that included the word "if."

– SUZANNE, daughter of Bill

"Never trust the federal government."

– MAC, father of Brian

"Three things you can live without: wet
toilet paper, warm beer, and a wise guy!"

– ROBERT, father of Lynda

"If you are going to work for yourself, you need
to have a daily dollar goal that meets your needs."

– JOHN, father of Brian

"Don't let your mouth write a
check your ass can't cash."

– BINO, father of Kristen

If my sibs and I ever asked our dad,
"Why?" he'd say, "Because Little
Willie likes cheesecake!"

– MERLE, daughter of Ron

"I used to look like a Greek god—
and now all I look like is a Greek."

– MURRAY, father of Elyse

"IF YOU HAVE A 50/50 CHANCE,
90 PERCENT OF THE TIME YOU
WILL BE WRONG."

– DEWEY, father of Joan

"I may have been born yesterday . . .
but I was downtown by 8:00."

– JERRY, father of Shawn

Whenever my dad got into a conversation
that became quite argumentative or
awkward, he would interject with,
"Think the rain will hurt the rhubarb?"

– SCOTT, son of Jack

"A lady never leaves the house without a girdle."

– BILL, father of Wells

"Never marry a woman
unless you look at her mother,
because that's who you'll be
married to in forty years."

– ALFRED, father of Robert

"I only like two kinds of pie: hot and cold."

– DON, father of Donna

"NEVER MARRY FOR MONEY. JUST HANG OUT WITH A LOT OF RICH PEOPLE AND FALL IN LOVE."

– HOWARD, father of Benjamin

"You're only as good as your equipment."

– COURTENAY, father of Annie

Every Father's Day and birthday, I would call Dad in the morning to wish him a happy day and give an ETA when my sister and I would be arriving. He'd always say, "I hope you will have to ring the bell with your elbows." He hoped our arms would be so full of gifts we wouldn't be able to hit the doorbell with our hands.

– ELISSA, daughter of Arthur

My dad gave me some advice before a concert back when I was in high school: "Don't break more than one law at a time, and don't buy drugs from people you don't know."

– CAM, son of Ed

"Never eat a jelly donut in the greenroom before going on television."

– Author JOHN CHEEVER, father of Susan

To my first girlfriend on my first date (we needed a ride to the movies), my father used the same line he'd evidently "impressed" my mother with when they'd first met: "Did you comb your hair tonight . . . with an eggbeater?"

– MICHAEL, son of Sam

Whenever my sister or I would ask our dad if he'd seen my mom recently, he'd tell us to check the roof.

– MEREDITH, daughter of Rich

My grandfather didn't allow water at the breakfast table, just to torture his sons, who had often been out partying the night before. He'd see them all straggle in on a Saturday or Sunday morning and say, "I know my sons never drink at night, because they're always so thirsty in the morning."

— BETSY, granddaughter of James

"BE GOOD OR BE CAREFUL."

— DOMINIQUE, father of Michele

"I like your shirt. Did you buy it new?"

— ARTHUR, father of Allan

My dad's standard parting words:
"Don't drink in any strange toilets."

— BRAD, son of Hal

"It never hurts to wave!"

– FRED, father of Ali

"An ice-cream cone always lasts
longer than a hot date."

– WEB, father of Kiki

My late father always finished a dispute about
politics with some version of this lesson:
"Do you know what the definition of a
communist (liberal/democrat . . .) is? What's
mine is mine; what's yours is negotiable."

– BRIAN, son of Mac

"When you're dead, you're dead
for an awfully long time."

– BILL, father of Ann

"Frig 'em all 'cept six.
Save 'em for pallbearers."

– WES, father of Sam

"PEOPLE ARE CRAZIER
THAN ANYBODY."

– FRED, father of Dan

7

THE
SOFT
SPOT

Sure, he's always ready to cut off your allowance, ground you, or send you to your room with no dinner. But beneath that gruff exterior and his reputation as The Enforcer, there's a melting heart.

When I was in college, I would occasionally get a short note from my dad, typed on his business letterhead. It was rarely more than a couple of lines, usually saying something like, "We had dinner with the Hicks and can't wait for your spring vacation. We'll go shoot some pool." But the addendum was always the same, and it never got old. There would be a bit of currency stapled to the letter, and the P.S. would say, "I thought you would enjoy this picture of Andrew Jackson for your presidential portrait collection." Forty years later and I still think it's hilarious.

– ERIN, daughter of Jimmy

When I was rushing to get something done, Dad would say: "Peace . . . peace! Little steps for little feet." Not at all surprising coming from a United States Ambassador.

– ALYSON, daughter of Ronald

My father, providing consolation upon hearing of my broken heart: "You know, a woman I loved broke up with me, and I thought the world was over. And then I met your mother. That breakup was the best thing that ever happened to me."

– PADDY, daughter of George

Just before he walked me down the aisle, my dad said, "These special moments need to be remembered. Open your eyes and LOOK at everyone. Someday you will be glad for these memories."

– FAITH, daughter of Pete

"The universe is full of magical things, waiting for our wits to grow sharper."

– MATT, father of Sarah

My dad's way of telling me to "go get 'em" is to say, "Knock 'em dead, Al!" Except that I'm an ICU nurse, so that's really not appropriate.

– ALLIE, daughter of Bob

"You want me to make you a ham sandwich?" has always been my dad's response to almost anything. Didn't matter if you had scraped your knee, had a headache, or needed a new kidney—and all those things happened in our house. Always a ham sandwich. I have never even liked ham.

– MARTHA, daughter of Dan

"Dawn is the best part of the day."

– TOM, father of Lisa

"You'll always be my baby."

– LEO, father of Mary Elizabeth

One of my father's rituals was the morning phone check-in with his two children. He managed to be intensely interested in our lives without prying or meddling. He just wanted to chat: "What did your day look like? Did you catch the Yankees game last night? What did you think of that editorial in the *Times*?" Implicit in the outreach was an offer to provide guidance, if needed.

I lived in New York, where he grew up. He and my mother lived outside of Washington, DC. Part of the daily ritual was touching base with a city that he still intensely loved and missed. Those calls were a great anchor to me. I used them, more than I like to admit, to rant about a particular job where I felt underappreciated. When I paused to catch my breath, I'd hear a soft chuckle followed by, "Only thirty-five more years of work." That job lasted a while. The rants continued. Eventually he shortened the observation to "Only thirty-five more years . . ."

– SUSAN, daughter of Arthur

DAD WOULD ALWAYS
CAUTION US ABOUT OUR
FRIENDS OR BOYFRIENDS:
"DON'T LET HIM TREAT
YOU LIKE A SIDE ORDER
OF FRENCH FRIES."

– KATIE, daughter of Mark

8

THE SPORTING LIFE

Larger than life is how our fathers seem to us as kids. Then, even when we're grown, they have a certain something that makes us think, "What a sport." Here's to you, Dad.

Our dad is a competitive amateur golfer, and some of life's lessons result from his time on the course. So when it comes to either playing a sport or work, his advice is always, "Keep quiet and let your game/work do the talking."

— JENNIE AND JAMES, daughter and son of Phil

"Don't drink beer, drink vodka— your mother can't smell it."

— JOE, father of Joe

My dad was coach of the high school football team, so his advice was often sports-oriented: "You never have to explain a victory and you never can satisfactorily explain a defeat."

— DAVID, son of Joe

IN HIS WILL, MY FATHER SAID:
"LIVE EXTRAVAGANTLY.
TAKE TAXIS."

– NOEMI, daughter of Henri

When my sister and I were quite small,
my dad would have us recite a common
rhyme with a bit of a twist at the end.
We were naive enough to comply!

"There was a little girl who had a little curl,
Right in the middle of her forehead.
And when she was good, she was very, very good,
And when she was bad she was popular!"

And then we would curtsy to smiles and applause.

– DORSEY, daughter of Ed

I was an only child, and my dad had blinders on as far as I was concerned—I could do no wrong. He was an avid golfer ("A hacker!" he'd tell everyone), and when I reached my teens I was eager to join him. Alas, golf wasn't my game; I just didn't seem to have what it takes. But Dad still found something positive to say: "You've got a sweet little swing!" he'd crow, as the ball once more bounced into the rough. Naturally, we laughingly began to use it as the catchphrase any time I tried, and perhaps failed, at something new. In retrospect, not a bad way to coach a child.

– ERIN, daughter of Jim

"Old enough to know better but too young to care."

– JOHN, father of John

"The only way to swim is to swim fast."

– MARTY, father of Shelley

"I DON'T UNDERSTAND THESE PEOPLE WHO LEAVE THE BEACH AT 5:00 P.M. THEY'RE MISSING THE BEST PART!"

– RICHARD, father of Deb

In the summertime my dad would often say to me, "Taber, it doesn't get any easier."

Always said as we turned onto the main road from the public beach stop sign and a hot bikini'd babe sauntered by.

– TABER, son of Dick

When I was very little and learning to ride my bike, Dad (who cycled for the English team waaaaay back) used to tell me, "You have to fall off seven times before you can be a good cyclist," knowing full well that I couldn't count to seven! He's nearly eighty now, and still knocking out sixty miles on a Sunday bike ride.

– ANT, son of Mike

My dad is single these days and interested in meeting his match. He reported this exchange: "Someone once asked me how the pigeon shooting was going. I replied, 'Oh, no no no. I'm only after ruffed grouse.'"

– LYDIA, daughter of Taber

"I JUST TRY TO COOL."

– GEORGE, father of Eric

9

THE
GREAT
PROTECTOR

If you took a step in the wrong direction, hung out with the wrong crowd, hadn't invested your money right, who's there to put you back on the right track? Oh, yeah—and heaven forbid another kid tried to get in your face.

Our dad was the epitome of optimism. Every Sunday between Memorial Day and Labor Day, he would pile all eleven of us (he and my mom, nine kids, sometimes aunts as well) onto a twenty-three-foot sailboat and head out for lunch and swimming off the boat. Inevitably, there would be no wind and lots of fog. He didn't like to use his little outboard unless there was an emergency, so a couple of hours into the trip, we would all start complaining. He always reassured us by saying, "The fog will burn off, the sun will come out, and the wind will pick up—stick with me, kid!" Much to our amazement, he was always right. After he passed, one of our brothers had bumper stickers made with that advice printed on them—it's the best advice we know.

– ANN, MARY, TED, BARBARA, JOAN, CHUCK, DELIA, NATALIE, AND MOLLY, children of Dick

My father always urged me to go to college. He said, "I don't want you to end up slinging hash."

– SANDY, daughter of Herb

Whenever I was about to do something foolish or dangerous—or something, I suppose, that simply displeased my father—he would say, "Don't let a little fear and common sense stop you."

– TODD, son of Ron

My father on all of his children:
"Between the hell of their living
and the fear of their dying,
there's never a dull moment."

– OLIVE, daughter of Tom

Before anything fraught with possible poor judgment, from waterskiing to going out on a Saturday night as teenagers, my father would caution: "Be sure you take a smart pill."

– AIDAN, son of Doug

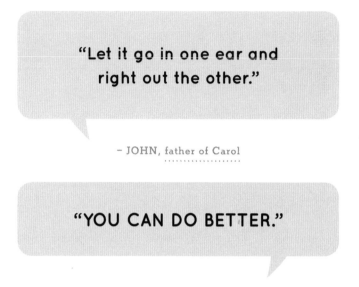

"Let it go in one ear and right out the other."

– JOHN, father of Carol

"YOU CAN DO BETTER."

– MARTY, father of Shelley

I can recall my father coming to tuck me in each night. After he kissed me goodnight and turned off the light, as he was closing the door, he would always turn and say to me, "I love you more than life itself."

– AMY, daughter of Bob

My father has always said, "Be smart, don't be stupid." You live, you learn, and while I was definitely living, nothing resonated in my mind as much as the thought of "being stupid," because I don't like that word and I consider myself an intelligent person.

Both of my parents gave me a lot of freedom and tremendous support in my formative years, and hearing that line every time I left the house has left its mark in almost all my decision making. So much so that I now have BSDBS tattooed on my forearm. We can always get ourselves in a bad situation: I did and continue to all the time. But being smart in a bad situation can be the difference between making it home that night, and putting yourself and others in harm's way.

I recently turned twenty-eight, and now instead of saying, "BSDBS," he says, "Read your tat." I hear his voice loud and clear every time.

– CAITLIN, daughter of Rick

> "BE CAREFUL WITH THE PARTYING, BECAUSE ONCE YOU'RE A PICKLE YOU CAN'T EVER BE A CUCUMBER AGAIN."

– JOHN, father of Marisa

"Don't ever play dumb. A man who doesn't love you for your brain isn't worth your time."

– RICHARD, father of Meredith

"The moment you think you want to change someone you love, dump 'em. You don't like them for the right reasons and they won't change anyway!"

– DOUG, father of Charlotte

Whenever we were leaving the house growing up, whether it was off to college or even just to go out for the night, my dad always said the same thing when he said good-bye: "OK now, nothin' crazy!" He believes this to be an all-encompassing warning, regardless of the situation. So, a couple of years ago, when I opened a fun gift and clothing store, what do you think I called it? You got it: Nothin' Crazy.

– ERIN, daughter of Bill

"WHAT OTHER PEOPLE THINK OF YOU IS NONE OF YOUR BUSINESS."

– CHARLIE, father of Lisa

"Don't come into my yard and honk expecting me to come out and greet you!"

– DON, father of Mary

ON THE OCCASION OF LEARNING HOW TO DRIVE: "WHY ARE YOU SPEEDING UP FOR A RED LIGHT?"

– BILL, father of Mary

Most mornings when I was very young, my dad drove me to school. Knowing that my mom was watching us through the kitchen window as we made our way to the garage, my dad would say, "Let's SKIP!" So, my 5'10" suited and hatted father and I would hold hands and skip like little girls all the way to the car, giggling. I never figured out (Mom had to tell me years later) that he did it because he was self-conscious about a small limp he had, the result of a car accident. Didn't he know how much she loved that limp? It's what kept him out of the army, safe and sound, until they met.

Wish I'd not outgrown the skipping ("Oh, *Dad*") or the rides to school so quickly. By the time I was twelve, he was memory. He also used to dress all in black and follow me and my friends from the other side of the street when we went trick-or-treating, so as not to embarrass me.

– LAURA, daughter of Jimmy

My dad had a "Some Rule," which
is financial advice to live by:

"Some in the bank,

some in stocks,

some in real estate, and

some under the mattress."

– ELLEN, daughter of Roswell

"Hold down the fort!"

– GEORGE, father of Ann

"There's always a faster gun." This one was usually said in the context of anyone expressing heartbreak that someone else was better than they were at X. Dad is very into trying your very hardest, but not being a poor sport when someone is just plain better at it than you are.

– NICHOLE, daughter of Ron

I would obsess over projects and homework, and my dad would finally get me to stop by saying, "Perfect is the enemy of good."

– JAY, son of Jeff

"Pay attention while I am alive, don't weep over my grave when I am dead."

I did . . . and I don't.

– FAITH, daughter of Peter

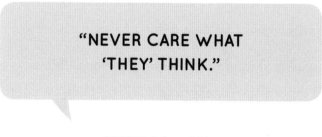

"NEVER CARE WHAT 'THEY' THINK."

– LENNY, father of Lizzz

"Don't drive so close to the parked cars. If you scrape a car driving on the other side, you have a prayer of saying they were over the line. If you hit a parked car, there's not much of a defense."

– HENRY, father of Meredith

Two takes on dog poop:

"Don't cutcha foot."

– LEO, father of Suzy

"Don't step on the umpapa."

– TOM, father of Olive

"ENJOY THE SIGHTS—
DON'T BECOME ONE."

– BINO, father of Kristen

10

LOVE
AND
FAMILY

You'll hear it over and over as life goes on: "Nothing's more important than family." Too true—and dads are at the center of it all.

It was a Palm Sunday dinner, and my first time meeting most of my now-wife's primarily Italian family. Her father took me aside and said, "All right, here's how you make these things easier on yourself: Eat the antipasti and all the snacks they put out. When we sit down for the meal, say yes to everything. Everyone will be staring at your plate. When they offer you seconds, and they will, you say, 'Yes, please.' When they offer you thirds, you say, 'Yes, I'd love some more of that.' When they ask if you want to take some home with you, you say, 'Yes, give me as much as you can give me.' There's no use saying no. They'll give it to you anyway."

– JEFF, son-in-law of Norm

When I came out to my mom and dad in 1978, my dad said, "You are such a good man and more of a man than any I know. I am so proud of you. There will be people that don't understand, but I do and I love you."

– RANDY, son of J.D.

My father is kind of a John Wayne type who will say, "Only the best for my hogs" after he's done something really sweet for his daughters.

– ANNIE, daughter of Courtenay

When I was a little girl I was extremely skinny. My father used to say that if I grew hair on my chest and stood sideways, I would look like a pipe cleaner.

– MARGIE, daughter of Arthur

My dad was a lifelong military man—both Army and Marines. As I neared my eighteenth birthday, he said, "Don't even think of joining the military. No daughter of mine will ever be treated like a second-class citizen."

– KACI, daughter of Paul

When I was in my second month of college freshman year at a two-year school for young ladies, I was expelled for abusing my parietal privileges (i.e., I had a male in my room after visiting hours). I received this news in the college president's office, and was instructed to ring up my parents and let them know of this revolting development . . . in front of the president. To my **GREAT** relief, no one was home and I was told I could leave and make the call from my dorm. I did, and upon hearing the news my mother said, "Just you wait until your father gets home, young lady!" He was away on business, as he usually was during any family crisis.

I saw my father walk up to our back door a few days later when he returned. He opened the door, took one look at me, and said, "Not a good move, Oiseau (my nickname)." Period.

The next day he told me to give my b.f. a call and invite him to the house. I did.

– MARTHA, daughter of Tom

"YOU CAN CHOOSE TO BE MARRIED OR YOU CAN CHOOSE TO BE SINGLE, BUT YOU CANNOT BE BOTH AT THE SAME TIME."

– CASEY, father of Charlie

Whenever my dad was asked what he wanted by his three kids (birthday, Christmas, Father's Day, etc.), he always answered, "Good kids." It was kind of frustrating—didn't he just want a tie?—but he did end up with three "good kids."

– BARBI, daughter of Karl

My brothers, sister, and I were pretty rough-and-tumble kids. Whenever my mother or grandmother (who was very prim and proper) would start twittering about how filthy they were getting, my dad would say, "Relax—every kid should eat a pound of dirt before they die."

– WILL, son of Rea

Dad's sarcastic nickname for my loquacious mother was always "The Clam" since, he said (lovingly), "She never shuts her shell!"

– BOB, father of Nancy

My dad's general address for gathering his three girls to his side: "Where are my troops?"

– JULIE, daughter of Greg

Until we were in middle school, my sister and I would race to the door the second my dad got home from work, rattling off all our daily happenings. He mostly loved the assault, but some days when he was tired, he'd cry out, "Confound it, girls! Can't I get my hind leg in the door first?"

— DONNA, daughter of Don

My dad's older brother Jim and his wife used to ask my parents to get together all the time. They've always been close, but their son was much older than we kids were. So Jim would call and say, "Let's take the boat out Friday night!" "Can't," my dad would say. A couple of weeks later, he'd say, "I have Red Sox tickets Saturday evening—how about it?" "Sorry," my dad would say. This went on and on until my dad finally said, "Jim, I don't think you guys understand. I have to stay home on the weekends to wait for the police to call!"

— ELIZABETH, daughter of Bill

That voice.

"Howyadoin? What'sitmakeadifference?"

His first impression was that of a mobster. It was my father who'd go into the local Barnes & Noble and say, in that raspy ridiculous voice, "Yes, I'm wondering if you have the new Brad Meltzer book? He's my favorite author in the world!" And the clerk would say, "Mr. Meltzer . . . we know he's your son. We know."

And I remember when my second book came out and my father was going in for hip replacement surgery. I go into his room . . . and he's totally out of it. He's filled with tranquilizers and all the anesthetic . . . and he opens his eyes . . . he has no idea where he is, and he says, "I love you." And then he says, "I sold a dozen books up there." And I said, "That's what you're thinking of when you're this close to death? That's what you're thinking of?" And I asked him, "Did you tell them about the paperbacks?"

– Author BRAD MELTZER, son of Stu

My father was French-Canadian, so whether or not his bilingualness had anything to do with this funny little phrase, I don't know. But now my own kids and grandchildren say it, too. Whenever anything is pleasing—the weather, a good meal, an unexpected little something that happened in the day—he would say, "Nice, nice, beautifully nice!"

– TESSIE, daughter of Jules

WHEN I WAS AROUND, OH, TWO YEARS OLD, MY DAD STARTED TO SAY, "I PITY THE MEN YOU MARRY."

– MEREDITH, daughter of Don

When I was a very young child, my father created a regular routine that I loved and remember well years later. When he arrived home at the end of the day, we'd greet him at the door, and every time he'd ask who we were and pretend not to know us. Then he and my mother would have a drink while she prepared dinner and they would talk about his day and hers. While they chatted, my father would lift my sister and I up to sit on top of the fridge. We sat still and quiet, as it was both exciting and scary to be up there!

When I think of it now, I realize it was pretty creative of him. My sister and I thought he was so cool for putting us there, and he and my mother had this very civilized little part of the day together.

Thanks, Dad, for all the nutty things you did.

– LEE, daughter of Leo

My father concludes every note he has ever sent me with, "Love you forever and ever no matter what." Even when he texts me he signs off with "LUFE&ENMW - LD."

— HILARY, daughter of Peter

ASK
YOUR
MOTHER

We've heard it all our lives. Is it a pass-the-buck kind of thing, or deferring to greatness? Perhaps we'll never know . . .

"I don't want to get yelled
at by your mother."

– MICHAEL, father of Amy

The thing my dad always told me (that I never listened to): "Your life would be so much easier if you do what I do, and just always do whatever your mother tells you instead of arguing with her."

– AMY, daughter of Randolph

"I think your mother better
take over the driving lessons."

– HENRY, father of Meredith

Whenever my dad thought maybe he shouldn't make a decision on his own (and perhaps have to suffer the repercussions) he'd always say, "I'd better check with the Boston office." And that would be my mother.

– ERIN, daughter of Jimmy

ON ANY GIVEN SATURDAY
OR SUNDAY: "IF YOU
WANT TO HELP DADDY,
GO HELP MOMMY."

– LESLIE, daughter of Al

12

"OH, DAD!"

How many times have you said that in your life out of embarrassment, frustration, exasperation—and, once in a while, even out of joy? It's a sentiment that never gets old, no matter if you're rolling your eyes or not.

Many years ago I reluctantly moved to a resort town so small and quiet that you could roll a bowling ball down Main Street for six months of the year and not hit a soul. I called and told my dad, who said, "Well, it's not the end of the world. But you could see it from there."

– ANN, daughter of Greg

In the sixties, when my brothers would bring their long-haired "hippie" friends home to dinner, my father would sit at the end of the dining room table and ask, "So, any news on the barber strike?" An embarrassment every time.

– AMY, daughter of Jim

"Not enough time in the day? So get up an hour earlier!" (And he did . . .)

– MAX, father of Jean

"How many jobs are you working? Only two???"

– TODD, father of Chessy

"If you're not bleeding, you're not hurt."

– BOB, father of Catherine

"THE EARLY BIRD GETS THE WORM, BUT THE SECOND RAT GETS THE CHEESE."

– ED, father of Joelle

"I brought you into this world and I can take you out of it and make another one who looks just like you."

– STEVE, father of Shane and Kolton

When he heard that someone had died, my father would always say, "First time?"

– ANN, daughter of Nick

Dropping me at college for the first time my freshman year, Dad imparted his final words of wisdom on his way out of my dorm room: "Try to change your sheets every now and then." And I still try to change my sheets every now and then.

– MICHELLE, daughter of Carl

EVERY TIME I WALKED
INTO A ROOM AND SAID,
"OH, GOD!" HE'D SAY,
"JUST DAD WILL DO."

– EMILY, daughter of Dick

"YOU CAN BE REPLACED BY A RESPECTFUL CHILD."

— DICK, father of Emily

There were a lot of us in our house, so when someone got sick, the warning went out. My father would exclaim, "There's a fungus among us!"

— OLIVE, daughter of Tom

"Don't forget to call." Before cell phones, when the dreaded long-distance charges were still exorbitant, my father always wanted us to call home by ringing the phone once and then hanging up when we got to our destination. That was how he knew we had arrived safely.

— PATRICIA, daughter of Joe

When I was in my midthirties, had no serious boyfriend, and felt my biological clock ticking, I decided to broach the subject of single parenthood with my parents: "What would you think if I were to find a sperm donor and had a baby in the next year or so?" My father turned to me with an impassive face and said, "I wouldn't think anything because I would be dead."

– CHRIS, daughter of Andy

When we were lazy or complaining about weeding jobs and other chores, Dad would say, "Were you born when there was a strike on?"

– NIFFY, daughter of Tom

My dad always said you need to know the proper names of tools. He would bring his toolbox in the living room and my brother and I had to properly identify the tools he pulled out of the box. His version of flash cards.

– TIM, son of Glenn

"You know what's wrong with you Millennials? You require too much positive reinforcement."

– TODD, father of Chessy

WHEN WE KIDS WERE SURPRISED AT MY DAD'S YOUTHFUL EXPERIENCES: "DID YOU THINK I WAS BORN OLD?"

– RAUL, son of Raul

"IF YOU AREN'T EARLY THEN YOU'RE LATE, BECAUSE YOU ONLY HAVE SIXTY SECONDS TO BE 'ON TIME.'"

– JIM, father of Debbie

I guess there's a whole bunch of people who are too young to get this, but back in the day, you could play a song on a jukebox for only five cents. Whenever I'd get revved up—which was all the time—my father would look at me and say, "Who put a nickel in you?"

– MARTHA, daughter of Greg

Me: "Dad . . . I really hate Tommy for pushing me around."

Dad: "Careful how you use the word "hate"—it's a pretty strong word."

I've never used that word the same way since.

– DAN, son of Clare

Before we'd get in the car, even if it was just a trip to the grocery store: "Everyone, empty your bladders!"

– MARISA, daughter of John

"Never trust a man that doesn't wear a
belt or can't shine his own shoes."

– AL, grandfather of Lorraine

"HERE, LET ME SHOW
YOU HOW TO DO THIS."

– TODD, father of Francesca

"There's nothing a Dairy Queen
hot fudge sundae can't cure."

– RICHARD, father of Deb

If I fell or otherwise hurt myself—
but not seriously—my dad would say,
"Don't bleed on the carpet."

– ELLEN, daughter of Bob

My dad, a captain in the United States Navy, greeted us every morning with, "Rise and shine! Another day in which to excel!"

Just as groan-inducing as you might imagine. This was sometimes accompanied by the musical stylings of the Mormon Tabernacle Choir or Whitney Houston's rendition of "The Star-Spangled Banner."

– SUSAN, daughter of Jim

"All verbals must be in writing."

– RICHARD, father of Alexander

Daddy used to say about people who lived beyond their means or who were show-offy, "Fly high, land on a turd."

– SARA, daughter of Bobby

"Wash your language."

– JIM, father of Joan

Whenever he answered the phone and it was for one of us kids, my father would say, "Mimi? Mimi Kavanaugh? Star of stage, screen, radio, and TV?" Much of the time the caller would be baffled—Dad didn't care if it was a friend, a date, a relative, he just thought it got funnier and funnier. And it kind of did. And now, occasionally, I use it myself.

– MIMI, daughter of Bud

"Turn off the lights, Mr. Edison is rich enough."

– ALDO, father of Judy

My Marine father would wake us kids up in the morning—frequently by unceremoniously dumping us out of our bunk beds onto the floor— with, "Attack the dawn!"

– GREG, son of Irving

Any time I'd go out to a party, when I'd come home my dad would say, "Did you meet anyone you like better than yourself?"

– ANN, daughter of Jack

ACKNOWLEDGMENTS

First and always, I want to thank my team at Abrams, more family than workmates, including top dog and dear friend Michael Jacobs; longtime colleague and helpmate Mary Wowk; my resilient, clever, and utterly delightful editor, David Cashion; the ever-patient John Gall; puzzle-solving designer Devin Grosz; and the entire marketing, design, and sales machine that makes publishing with Abrams a slam-dunk joy.

It's unusual to tip your hat in a book's acknowledgments to strangers, but that's just what I've got to do here. So many of the people—and their dads—who shared the quips and stories that appear in these pages are folks I'll never meet. But every reader of *Like My Father Always Said . . .* will visit with a lot of new people and hear, identify with, and smile at their stories. Truly, I bow to you all, friends and strangers both, for putting you and your father out there. Thanks for the memories.

ABOUT THE AUTHOR

Erin McHugh is a former publishing executive and the award-winning author of more than twenty books of trivia, history, children's titles, and more, including *One Good Deed: 365 Days of Trying to Be Just a Little Bit Better* and *Like My Mother Always Said* . . . She lives in New York City. She is the daughter of James Francis McHugh.